A Guide to Conducting Integrated Baseline Reviews (IBR)

Applicable to All Projects Applying Project Controls

Association for Project Management

Association for Project Management
Ibis House, Regent Park
Summerleys Road, Princes Risborough
Buckinghamshire
HP27 9LE

British Library Cataloguing in Publication Data is available.
Paperback ISBN: 978-1-903494-49-3
eISBN: 978-1-903494-53-0

Cover design by Fountainhead Creative Consultants
Typeset by RefineCatch Limited, Bungay, Suffolk
in 11/14 pt Foundry Sans

Contents

Contents

Figures and tables

Figures

Tables

Foreword

Projects exist to deliver change. Government projects are about getting things done to help transform society and the way government works. The range of projects is diverse and exciting: from new hospitals or rail networks, to innovative IT systems and transformational change. Projects require substantial investment; the whole life cost of the Government Major Projects Portfolio (GMPP) alone is about £500bn, and there is huge potential to deliver these projects more efficiently and more effectively.

I have worked in and around major projects for 30 years and, in my experience, success comes down to having the experience and confidence to make sound judgements to consistently 'do the right project right'. Having highly skilled and motivated project delivery professionals equipped with knowledge of what works will help us implement projects well and deliver excellence.

To improve the delivery performance of major projects, we need to learn from previous experience. This can be achieved by looking for patterns, for example, are we consistently finding the same issue in projects? Unfortunately, I often find that we fail to learn – or apply – the lessons of the past. For example, the conditions for project success are often set right at the very outset. Aspects for consideration include whether all the scope has been included in the baseline, whether risks and uncertainties have been identified, whether the project has an appropriate mix of resources and whether a suitable management control process has been implemented. It is good practice to check, and ensure, these are in place from the very earliest stages of the project, regardless of the project size or complexity.

This guide focuses on integrated baseline reviews (IBR) but the principles it follows are applicable to other types of review. The intent of the IBR is to look at the process as a whole to see if it is working as intended and to improve confidence that the information you are using to make decisions is reliable. The book guides the reader through the review process, suggesting what the review should be looking for, and how the output should be used not only to improve the project under review, but rather how outputs can be collated to prevent common issues from reoccurring.

Tim Banfield
Director, Strategy
Major Projects Authority
Cabinet Office

Preface

This document is based on a Ministry of Defence (MoD) Document – *A Guide to the Integrated Baseline Review Process* – first issued in October 2002. The MoD kindly gave permission for APM to make use of this guide. The original document was based on best practice, was developed over a period of time by various contributors and it became specific to the requirements of the MoD. The APM Planning, Monitoring and Control (PMC) Specific Interest Group (SIG) has reviewed and updated the guide to improve its clarity, applicability and accessibility resulting in this pan-sector, pan-industry version, whilst adhering to the original guide's intent.

Stephen Jones
Chairman APM Planning, Monitoring and Control
Specific Interest Group

Acknowledgements

A *Guide to Conducting Integrated Baseline Reviews* was developed by a sub-committee of the Association for Project Management's Planning, Monitoring and Control Specific Interest Group, consisting of:

Alan Bye	Programme management specialist, Rolls-Royce
Breda Ryan	Project controls manager, Jacobs
Ewan Glen	Principal consultant, BMT Hi-Q Sigma
Stephen Jones	Deputy head of project management capability, Sellafield Ltd

The APM Planning, Monitoring and Control SIG is most grateful to BAE Systems, Rolls-Royce, BMT Hi-Q Sigma, Harmonic Ltd, R & N.R. Consulting Limited, Sellafield Ltd, Jacobs, General Dynamics and the Ministry of Defence and Industry partners who made their Review Guides available to the SIG that formed the base from which this pan-sector, pan-industry version was developed.

In addition, contributions were received from the wider members of the PMC SIG and volunteers from a number of industry sectors who supported the development of the document, including providing invaluable input throughout the review process.

The authors would like to thank all for their help in creating this guide.

Applicability

This handbook provides guidance on the conduct of an individual review in the context of the overall integrated baseline review (IBR) process, a formal process conducted to assess the content and integrity of the baseline against which project performance will be measured.

The guide offers an IBR overview for projects and their customers, describing the activities, planning and training prior to the start of the review, the review responsibilities and criteria for the review team, and guidance for the review of information.

Guidance is intended to be applied to projects of all sizes in all industry sectors. The IBR process should be scaled and tailored to the project concerned.

IBRs are typically conducted in environments utilising earned value management to ensure that the baseline that underpins the performance data is robust, but all projects can benefit from this type of baseline review to check the validity and robustness of their project controls environment.

This handbook may be used in conjunction with APM's *Earned Value Management Compass* [1] with which it shares many common attributes and the goal of having a single source of truth and better informed decision making.

Each business may apply different terminology to that described in this document and as such should apply sensible judgement to the intent of the review.

1

Introduction

An integrated baseline review (IBR) is the process of performing a technical and schedule review to establish a balanced understanding of the planning maturity of the project. The IBR will review:

- the project management plan;
- the methods and metrics used to measure contract performance or progress;
- the management control processes that operate during the project's execution;
- the technical merits of the schedule;
- the risk associated with the baseline.

The purpose of the IBR is to achieve and maintain a project and understanding of the risks inherent in the performance measurement baseline (PMB) and the management control processes that will operate during its execution.

The process involves a review of documentation, an on-site review of the project's proposed planning and management systems, and identifies follow-up actions as necessary to ensure that the baseline has matured to an acceptable level.

Integrated baseline reviews are not to be confused with audits. An audit looks in depth for conformance to a standard or procedure, whereas an IBR is looking for assurance that your baseline is robust, the entire process is operating as it should and you are in control. The IBR should be seen as a precursor to successful project delivery.

The guidance within this document is geared around an initial full review. It is also applicable to subsequent reviews such as demonstration and surveillance reviews [2, 4]. It is expected, however, that subsequent reviews will generally be of smaller scale than the initial, and the guidance within this handbook should be tailored as required.

Self-assessment is an important part of any pre-review activity, and this guide should be used in support of that process. It contains what could be called 'the exam questions', and the project manager should use these to identify the potential findings or gaps to determine if the project is 'ready' for the review. The *EVM Compass* [1] is recommended as a good practice process to support self-assessment. The self-assessment should be shared with key stakeholders before the review starts because this may raise areas the review team may wish to focus on. A gap analysis between the two should be part of the post review activities.

It is important to agree terms of reference for the review, which are approved by the review sponsor in advance of the review.

An IBR is not an opportunity to give a colleague a grilling or criticise someone's work. Reviews should be constructive and independent. The review team constitutes a fresh set of eyes looking at a project, confirming what the project manager should have already known through self-assessment, and is character-istic of the good culture all projects should embrace. IBRs provide an opportunity to further improve the project baseline and control processes, giving the project a greater chance of success and promoting the characteristics of good project management culture.

2

Purpose

The purpose of an IBR is to achieve and/or maintain a project and customer understanding of the content of the performance measurement baseline (PMB), the risks inherent in the PMB, and the management control processes that will operate during the project's execution.

It should confirm that:

- the PMB incorporates the entire scope of the project;
- the work is scheduled to meet the project's objectives;
- risks are identified and are being managed;
- an appropriate amount and mix of skilled and experienced resources have been assigned to accomplish all requirements;
- suitable management control processes are being implemented.

The review should provide both the project and its customer the assurance that valid and timely performance data will be provided throughout the execution of the project. The output of the IBR should be reported via the existing project governance forums for considered decision making.

Any findings from the review that require a corrective action should be analysed for 'root cause', identifying whether the cause is specific to the project or systematic within the project delivery organisation. This will facilitate the identification of improvement initiatives, using Pareto Analysis for example, to identify where efforts will produce the greatest results. This may require a number of reviews, across a number of projects, to be performed before sufficient data are available. It is important to conduct root cause analysis as early as possible to maximise the opportunity for timely rectification.

3

IBR process summary

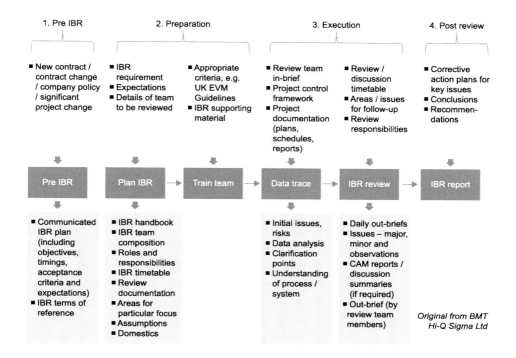

1. Pre IBR

- New contract / contract change / company policy / significant project change

2. Preparation

- IBR requirement
- Expectations
- Details of team to be reviewed

- Appropriate criteria, e.g. UK EVM Guidelines
- IBR supporting material

3. Execution

- Review team in-brief
- Project control framework
- Project documentation (plans, schedules, reports)

- Review / discussion timetable
- Areas / issues for follow-up
- Review responsibilities

4. Post review

- Corrective action plans for key issues
- Conclusions
- Recommen- dations

Pre IBR → Plan IBR → Train team → Data trace → IBR review → IBR report

- Communicated IBR plan (including objectives, timings, acceptance criteria and expectations)
- IBR terms of reference

- IBR handbook
- IBR team composition
- Roles and responsibilities
- IBR timetable
- Review documentation
- Areas for particular focus
- Assumptions
- Domestics

- Initial issues, risks
- Data analysis
- Clarification points
- Understanding of process / system

- Daily out-briefs
- Issues – major, minor and observations
- CAM reports / discussion summaries (if required)
- Out-brief (by review team members)

Original from BMT Hi-Q Sigma Ltd

4

Review timing

The project must be confident that the baseline is complete before holding the IBR.

The initial review is considered the most important as it seeks to achieve an understanding and agreement of the baseline from which performance data will be generated. It is beneficial to conduct the initial review as close as possible to the completion of the first reporting cycle after commencing the project. This is to ensure data is available for the review and thorough planning has been undertaken early in the project life cycle. An early review will provide the opportunity for timely completion of any rectification activities.

Subsequent reviews should be held when the review sponsor agrees that a review would be beneficial. These may be on a periodic basis, aligned with project/planning phases, or with pre-planned management reviews such as key stage gates (or similar).

The timing of subsequent reviews will be dependent upon a number of factors including:

- project duration;
- risk;
- complexity;
- project performance;
- change;
- customer requirement;
- company policy.

The duration of the review depends on the terms of reference, but can take anything from a few days up to two weeks; however, a typical review will last five days.

5

Roles and responsibilities

The following table outlines the roles and responsibilities of the various stake-holders involved in the integrated baseline review.

Table 1 Roles and responsibilities

Role	Responsibilities
Review sponsor (this may be a person internal or external to the organisation delivering the project)	Person who initiates the review, i.e. the review is conducted on behalf of the review sponsor. • Agree the objectives and schedule for the IBR process and supporting reviews • Ensure an adequate number of suitably qualified and experienced personnel are available to support the IBR process • Ensure issues resulting from reviews are resolved in a timely manner
IBR lead	The person leading the review on behalf of the review sponsor. • Ensure consistency of approach by the review team • Review and approve the IBR handbook • Deliver out-brief and IBR report
IBR facilitator	The person providing day-to-day management of the process on behalf of the IBR lead. • Provide technical direction and leadership • Assign responsibilities to review team members • Coordinate outputs from the review team • Ensure review team members are adequately trained and prepared for their review activities
Review team members	Everyone participating in the review working for the IBR lead. • Be prepared for the review and attend IBR training workshops • Familiarise themselves with the statement of work (SoW) prior to the review • Review the project's planning documentation and undertake data traces for their area of responsibility • Conduct interviews/discussions with project team members

(Continued)

Table 1 *Continued*

Role	Responsibilities
	▪ Provide a record of the documentation reviewed and an output from the interviews and data traces conducted, ready for inclusion into the final IBR report
Project manager	Responsible for delivery of the project. ▪ Provide a project lead
Project lead (this is often the project manager)	Point of contact from project being reviewed. ▪ Provide the appropriate planning documentation to the team for review prior to the start of the IBR ▪ Provide working space and support for the IBR review team ▪ Arrange schedules for interviews/discussions with relevant project personnel ▪ Deliver in-brief
Project team members	Everyone supporting/working on the project being reviewed. ▪ Make yourself available for discussions/interviews as per timetable

The IBR lead, facilitator and review team members should be independent of the project under review and may be independent of the organisation to add additional objectivity.

6

Overview of process

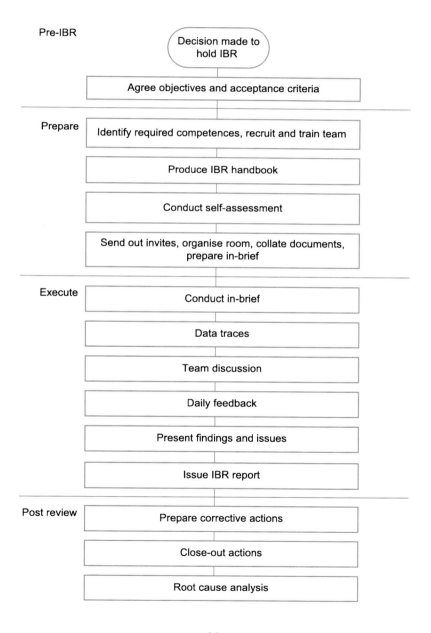

Pre-IBR

Decision made to hold IBR

Agree objectives and acceptance criteria

Prepare

Identify required competences, recruit and train team

Produce IBR handbook

Conduct self-assessment

Send out invites, organise room, collate documents, prepare in-brief

Execute

Conduct in-brief

Data traces

Team discussion

Daily feedback

Present findings and issues

Issue IBR report

Post review

Prepare corrective actions

Close-out actions

Root cause analysis

A Guide to Conducting Integrated Baseline Reviews (IBR)

The following tables describe the overall process for implementing an integrated baseline review. The numbers in the first columns refer to the steps in later chapters of this book.

Table 2 Pre-IBR

	Input	Process	Output	Responsibility
1.1	New contract / contract change / company policy / significant project change	Decision to hold an IBR	▪ Updated contract and project plan ▪ Terms of reference	Review sponsor
1.2	▪ IBR guide ▪ Contract	Agree objectives and acceptance criteria	▪ Communicate IBR plan (including objectives, timings, acceptance criteria and expectations)	IBR lead Project lead

Table 3 Preparation

	Input	Process	Output	Responsibility
2.1	▪ IBR plan	Identify required competencies Identify review team	▪ Review team identified, contact list prepared, roles and responsibilities agreed, arrangements put in place to bring in independent team members where required.	IBR lead Project lead
2.2	▪ IBR handbook template ▪ IBR plan	Produce draft IBR handbook	▪ Draft IBR handbook	IBR lead Project lead
2.3	▪ Review team members ▪ Project team members	Train teams as required	▪ Trained project and IBR team members	IBR lead Project lead

Table 3 *Continued*

	Input	Process	Output	Responsibility
2.4	■ Project team members ■ Draft IBR handbook ■ *EVM Compass* [1] ■ *Scheduling Maturity Model* [3]	Project conduct self-assessment	■ Actions list, including issues for resolution prior to the IBR	Project lead
2.5	■ Draft IBR handbook	Agree the IBR timetable, including interview schedule	■ Updated draft IBR handbook to include timetable	IBR lead Project lead
2.6	■ Draft IBR handbook	Organise the IBR, e.g. book rooms, issue invites, security etc.	■ IBR event organised	Project lead
2.7	■ Draft IBR handbook	Finalise and issue IBR handbook	■ Final IBR handbook	IBR lead Project lead
2.8	■ Final IBR handbook	Collate and issue documents to be reviewed	■ Documentation issued to review team	Project lead
2.9	■ Project documentation	Review and familiarise with documents	■ Review team prepared	IBR lead
2.10	■ Project documentation ■ Action list	Prepare in-brief presentation and process storyboard	■ In-brief ■ Storyboard	Project lead

Table 4 Execution

	Input	Process	Output	Responsibility
3.1	▪ In-brief ▪ Storyboard	Brief review team on current project control system status	▪ Fully briefed review team	IBR lead Project lead
3.2	▪ IBR documentation ▪ Final IBR handbook	Conduct data traces	▪ Highlighted potential issues or good practice	Review team members
3.3	▪ Highlighted potential issues ▪ CAM specific data ▪ Final IBR handbook	Project team discussions	▪ Highlighted issues or good practice	Review team members
3.4	▪ Highlighted issues or good practice ▪ Final IBR handbook	Collate and document findings	▪ Draft IBR report	Review team members
3.5	▪ Draft IBR report ▪ Final IBR handbook	Daily feedback sessions	▪ Project response to issues raised	Review team members
3.6	▪ Draft out-brief presentation ▪ Final IBR handbook	Produce presentation	▪ Out-brief presentation	Review team members
3.7	▪ Draft IBR report ▪ Out-brief presentation	Present key issues and findings	▪ Fully de-briefed output team	Review team members Project team members
3.8	▪ Draft IBR report ▪ Out-brief presentation	Prepare and issue IBR report	▪ IBR report	IBR lead

Table 5 Post review

	Input	Process	Output	Responsibility
4.1	▪ Final IBR report	Prepare corrective action plan	▪ Corrective action plan	Project team members IBR lead
4.2	▪ Corrective action plan	Close-out actions	▪ Fully signed corrective action plan	Project team members Review team members IBR lead
4.3	▪ Project self-assessment ▪ Final IBR report ▪ Corrective action plan	Root cause analysis	▪ Trend of reoccurring issues ▪ Initiatives to reduce future occurrence of common IBR findings	Review sponsor

Where appropriate, it may be necessary for the review sponsor to identify a schedule of future IBR, demonstration and surveillance reviews based on the findings of the review.

In order to support the continuous improvement of the IBR process, it is advisable to conduct a post review feedback, to review the process from the participants' point of view.

7

Pre-IBR

7.1 Step 1.1 Decision to hold an IBR

Ideally, the schedule of reviews will have been planned and agreed in advance; however, significant events that affect the project may also trigger the requirement for a review, as indicated in Chapter 4 Review timing.

The review sponsor will make the decision to hold an IBR based on the criteria. The review sponsor will ensure the need for an IBR is represented in the contract or project plan. If not amendments shall be made to the relevant documentation.

The review sponsor will produce terms of reference for the review, as per the example in Annex A.

7.2 Step 1.2 Agree objectives and acceptance criteria

As soon as the decision to conduct an IBR has been taken, the IBR lead and the review sponsor should agree and define the specific objectives and acceptance criteria for the review. This agreement may be documented in an initial draft of the project IBR handbook, which is produced by the project lead. The following list provides the typical IBR objectives; to assess the PMB the intent is to establish that the following has been achieved:

- Assumptions underlying the plan are reasonable and documented.
- Project requirements have been translated into appropriate breakdown structures and authorised through documents such as work breakdown structure (WBS) and statement of work (SoW).
- Project schedule key milestones are identified and reflect a logical flow to accomplish technical work scope.
- The project organisation is identified and a clear responsibility link to the WBS is shown, e.g. responsibility assignment matrix (RAM).

- The planned use of resources (budgets, facilities, personnel, skills etc.) reflects availability and is sufficient to accomplish the technical scope of work within schedule constraints over the entire performance period.
- Sub-contract effort and performance reporting is integrated to the level that is effective for project control.
- Earned value techniques applied are appropriate for the scope of work being undertaken in order that project performance data will accurately reflect project achievement during the entire performance period.

Having taken project specifics into account and agreed the IBR objectives, care should be exercised to ensure that all parties involved are aware of the approach to be taken in conducting the review.

In order to formalise the review, the IBR lead should prepare an IBR plan, which is communicated to team members and the contractor.

8

Preparation

8.1 Step 2.1 Identify required competencies and identify review team

The IBR lead and project manager should identify the review team members. It is required that the review team include (where possible) personnel independent of the project and ideally have cross-functional representation.

Reviews should be led by a suitably qualified representative to ensure that a comprehensive evaluation of the performance measurement baseline (PMB) is performed and that all project control aspects have been addressed and captured.

Review team members should comprise project control specialists, with support from the project's engineering and technical staff. Project staff should be knowledgeable on the subject matter being examined. All team members will be allocated specific areas of responsibility ideally associated with their field of expertise.

The following areas of discipline and/or experience are required:

- project management;
- planning;
- scheduling;
- project control;
- business management;
- sub-contract management;
- technical management;
- contract management;
- risk management;
- resource management.

The size of the team and duration of the review should be proportionate and aligned with the project size and complexity. This should be agreed by the review sponsor, IBR lead and the project lead with reference to the terms of reference.

8.2 Step 2.2 Produce draft IBR handbook

A draft IBR handbook covering all aspects from within this guide that are applicable to the review in question should be produced and distributed. This will ensure that everyone involved has a clear understanding of the expectations, how it will be undertaken and the timing of the review.

8.3 Step 2.3 Train teams as required

Joint training sessions should be held wherever practicable for all personnel involved in the review, either as a review team member or project team member. The intent of the training is to provide enough information for the team to mutually understand both the IBR process and the cost, schedule, technical and management processes that should be used on the project. When necessary, it may be appropriate to bring in external personnel for training and facilitation.

Training should be designed and delivered to support the objectives of the review as agreed by the IBR lead and project lead. The essential elements of the training should include the following:

- communication skills (interview/discussion techniques, active listening etc.);
- performing the review (data traces, collecting evidence, dealing with conflict etc.);
- recording and reporting (how to document findings and issues, i.e. being clear, concise and consistent).

8.4 Step 2.4 Project conduct self-assessment

To assist in the preparation of a review, a self-assessment should be conducted, using APM *EVM Compass* [1] or this guide. This may completely replicate the entire scope of the IBR, or may just focus on particular areas of concern raised by the review sponsor. The self-assessment will identify areas that require further development, the current and target system maturity and establish actions to address any issues prior to the IBR.

In order to prepare for the IBR and to ensure all participants fully understand the process and benefits of the IBR, coaching should be arranged by the project lead or review sponsor.

The project should undertake data tracing as part of a self-assessment to identify any potential problem areas that subsequently can be briefed to the review team members.

8.5 Step 2.5 Agree the IBR timetable including interview schedule

The draft IBR handbook should be updated to include a timetable. This will show the major IBR activities, which shall include:

In-brief

- In-brief for the review team members explaining the purpose of the review and providing the opportunity for the introduction of both review and project team members.
- An overview of the project – to familiarise the team with the project scope, content and context; to gain an understanding of the project controls framework (PCF) and its maturity.

Data traces

- The review of project planning data, including system data traces and review of the PCF or equivalent and any associated project directives or instructions that support the PCF.

Discussion

- Discussions with control account managers (CAM(s)) identifying the basis on which the plan was established, ensuring that resources have been allocated and that appropriate earned value techniques have been identified.
- Typically discussions will also be held with project management, programme management office (PMO), finance, commercial, senior management and other significant stakeholders.

Daily review team meetings

- Plan of the day. This is a stand-up meeting held at the start of the each day to finalise/amend the schedule of activities for the day, and discuss what should be achieved.
- Daily feedback. This is a meeting that is held at 'close of business' each day, which includes the following activities:
  - confirmation of completion of activities scheduled for the day;
  - confirmation of write-up reports of discussions conducted;
  - sharing of review team findings;
  - daily de-briefs.

Out-brief

- A joint exit briefing by the review team addressing the review findings.
- An exception report addressing the review team's concerns and findings. All concerns requiring resolution should be identified and, if not already resolved prior to completion of the IBR, the estimated dates for resolution should be agreed.

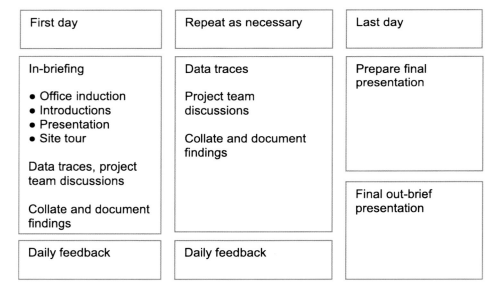

Figure 1 Typical review cycle

Reproduced with kind permission from the APM Planning, Monitoring and Control Specific Interest Group working group.

8.6 Step 2.6 Organise the IBR

The IBR will require a certain amount of administration in order to ensure the smooth conduct for the benefit of all stakeholders.

The project lead will typically arrange the following:

- Ensure that review team members are cleared for any access requirements, and that arrangements are in place for them to be collected/escorted whilst on site.
- Provide working space and support for the review team including a working area and administrative support as required.
- Schedule discussions with CAM(s) and other project management staff and ensure all personnel are available.
- Ensure that rooms for discussion are available – ideally the project's own work environment.

8.7 Step 2.7 Finalise and issue the IBR handbook

The draft IBR handbook should be finalised and issued to all stakeholders to ensure that they have an unambiguous understanding of the objectives, process and timetable for the review.

This is the responsibility of the IBR lead and project lead.

8.8 Step 2.8 Collate and issue documents to be reviewed

The following information should be provided to the review team members prior to the review to allow the team to familiarise themselves with it:

- statement of work;
- project management plan;
- work breakdown structure and dictionary;
- organisational breakdown structure;
- responsibility assignment matrix;

- project schedules, including top-level and lower-level schedules;
- outputs from risk analysis;
- risk register and opportunities log;
- project control framework (sometimes referred to as the earned value management system description);
- assumptions, exclusions, dependencies and constraints.

In addition the following documents may also be required:

- business case;
- work authorisation documents;
- signed control account plans or equivalent;
- change control documents (if appropriate);
- current and previous months performance reports (if available at the time of the first review);
- list of major suppliers;
- basic contract and modifications.

8.9 Step 2.9 Review and familiarise with documents

The review team members should familiarise themselves with project information provided in Step 2.8.

8.10 Step 2.10 Prepare in-brief presentation and process storyboard

Prior to the IBR the project should prepare an IBR in-brief and storyboard. The in-brief will provide an overview of the project and the processes it employs, typically identifying where any issues exist, as identified in Step 2.4. This should not compromise the progress of the review by focusing upon known issues.

The storyboard provides a visual representation of interactions between the various elements of the project control system.

9

Execution

The purpose of the review is to evaluate the robustness and suitability of the project control framework (PCF), the project controls environment and the project's compliance with it. The review provides assurance to the business that the PCF and processes are fully integrated and suitable for the size and complexity of the project.

The review provides the project team with an early independent check to validate the project's systems and baseline, and to enable continuous improvement initiatives.

9.1 Step 3.1 Brief IBR team members on current project control framework status

The in-brief is an opportunity for the review team members to gain an understanding of the project being reviewed and the PCF being operated within. The presenter should also highlight areas where the project may benefit from closer scrutiny with a view to obtaining potential solutions and guidance. In addition to presenting the in-brief presentation, this may include:

- office induction (e.g. tour of welfare facilities, health and safety information etc.);
- introductions to key staff;
- site tour (if appropriate).

9.2 Step 3.2 Data traces

Data tracing is an important component of any review and is a methodology for tracing a source data element through the PCF and understanding how the overall system operates.

Guidance on the conduct of data traces may be found in Annex B.

9.3 Step 3.3 Project team discussions

A key feature of the IBR is to conduct discussions in accordance with the agreed timetable and interview schedule (see Step 2.5 Agree the IBR timetable including interview schedule).

Discussions are held between the CAM and other significant stakeholders (with support from project team members if required) and review team members. This may be done in pairs, to allow one review team member to ask questions while the other makes notes.

Each discussion is scheduled for a maximum of two hours, including a short allowance for capturing the key issues identified.

Annex C provides discussion guidance and lines of enquiry that could be followed.

9.4 Step 3.4 Collate and document findings

Results of the discussions should be recorded and collated at the daily feedback session, to be incorporated into the review report.

Issues identified are categorised into those that require corrective action and those that are possible areas for improvement. It is advisable to prioritise the corrective actions into categories such as major and minor. These are to be discussed at the daily feedback session.

9.5 Step 3.5 Daily feedback sessions

It is beneficial to maintain a written record of the issues found during the review and to feed them back on a daily basis. This will provide all review team members with an overview of how the review is progressing and enable the project to clarify any issues, respond to the issues raised, and to prevent any 'surprises' at the out-brief.

9.6 Step 3.6 Produce presentation

Towards the end of the review an IBR out-brief presentation should be prepared to present the key issues and findings to the project team members and stakeholders.

9.7 Step 3.7 Present key issues and findings

After completion of a review, an IBR out-brief should be held with the project team members and stakeholders in order to present the key issues requiring corrective action, areas for possible improvement, and any good practices that should be shared.

9.8 Step 3.8 Prepare and issue final IBR report

Following the review the IBR lead will prepare a final IBR report that summarises the review. This includes, but is not limited to:

- the review participants' (review team plus project team staff engaged during the review) names and contact details;
- distribution list;
- the purpose and scope of the review;
- IBR lead overview;
- key issues requiring corrective action;
- areas of possible improvement;
- recommendations;
- lessons/learning from experience (LFE) on the conduct of the review.

10

Post review

10.1 Step 4.1 Prepare corrective action plan

The IBR lead should agree on a plan of actions to address each of the key issues raised in the IBR report with the project lead. The action plan should identify who is responsible for closing out the actions. The IBR lead reviews the adequacy of the proposed actions. The project lead is responsible for close-out of the corrective actions.

Areas of possible improvement identified in the IBR report should be resolved by the date agreed between the project lead and IBR lead.

Any additional risks/issues identified during the IBR are recorded in the risks/issues log and managed accordingly. The project lead should ensure that project team members have taken appropriate action to record these risks/issues.

10.2 Step 4.2 Close-out actions

A corrective action plan will be provided to identify the key issues raised in the IBR report; these will be closed out by the action owner. The IBR lead will sign off the action with the agreement of the review team member raising the action.

The review sponsor is accountable for ensuring that the actions are completed following the review.

10.3 Step 4.3 Root cause analysis

The review sponsor is responsible for ensuring root cause analysis is conducted for the self-assessment findings and the key issues raised in the IBR report.

The root cause of key issues and areas for improvement can be determined by using techniques like the '5 whys' and causal diagrams (e.g. Ishikawa diagrams).

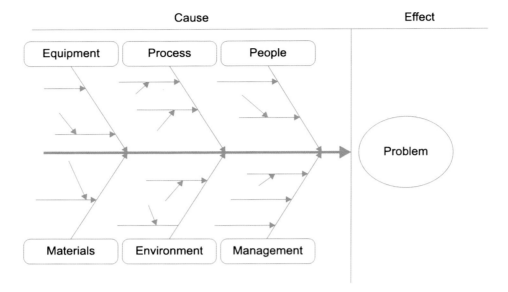

Figure 2 Causal diagram

Wikimedia Commons, a freely licensed media file repository.

The '5 whys' is an iterative questioning technique used to explore the cause-and-effect relationships underlying a particular problem. The primary goal of the technique is to determine the root cause of a defect or problem. The '5' in the name derives from an empirical observation on the number of iterations typically required to resolve the problem.

A coding system should be used to group the root cause descriptions into categories, for example behaviour, communication, document quality, planning etc. This will allow trending of common root causes across a number of projects, enabling initiatives to reduce future occurrences of common IBR findings.

Root cause trends should be prioritised using an appropriate methodology (e.g. Pareto) and reported on a 'score card' to highlight areas of concern.

Root cause	Count
Functions not engaged early	0
Unclear or complex wording	0
Documentation inadequate	0
Shortfall in training and/or experience	0
Inadequate resource	1
Internal team communication inadequate	1
Document format deficiencies	2
Lack of integrated team input	4
Inadequate assessment of personnel behaviour and performance	4
Underestimate/time allocation	6
Noncompliance with procedure	8
Risks not identified or appropriately assessed	15
Lack of questioning attitude	18
Standards not adequately communicated	40

Figure 3 Typical score card

Reproduced with kind permission from the APM Planning, Monitoring and Control Specific Interest Group working group.

11

Summary

An IBR is the process of performing a technical and schedule review to establish a balanced understanding of the planning maturity of the project. It should achieve and maintain a project and customer understanding of the risks inherent in the performance measurement baseline (PMB) and the management control processes that will operate during its execution. The review should also provide both the project and its customer the assurance that valid and timely performance data will be provided throughout the execution of the project.

The process involves a review of documentation, an on-site review of the project's proposed planning and management systems, and identifies follow-up actions as necessary to ensure that the baseline has matured to an acceptable level.

The guidance within this document is geared around an initial full review. It is also applicable to subsequent reviews such as demonstration and surveillance reviews. It is expected, however, that subsequent reviews will generally be of smaller scale than the initial one and the guidance within this handbook should be tailored as required.

Using this IBR guide will provide a standard and consistent approach to baseline reviews and support an improved approach to project delivery. The process will need to be applied iteratively and as required by your business and projects.

12

Annex A – Example terms of reference

Overview

Overview of project

(Should include brief description of project and a statement about the readiness for the review)

Purpose

What is the high-level purpose of this review?

What is the scope of the review?

Stakeholder

List the key review stakeholders

(See Table 1)

A Guide to Conducting Integrated Baseline Reviews (IBR)

What information is required for the review to fulfil its obligations?
(See Step 2.8 in Chapter 8)

Who is responsible for providing this information?

In what format should the information be provided?

When will the information for the review be available?

What information will be reported from the review?

To whom will this information be reported?

13

Annex B – Data traces

This section provides guidance on how the following data traces are undertaken:

- scope, organisation and authorisation;
- budget;
- schedule;
- labour;
- material;
- sub-contract management;
- earned value;
- managerial analysis;
- risk.

All documents shall be the latest approved version and made available for review when requested, typically this will be one week before.

13.1 Scope, organisation and authorisation

The scope, organisation and authorisation trace shows the progressive breakdown of a discrete piece of scope from the contract to at least the control account (CA) and usually to a lower level.

It is suggested that the following documents should be reviewed:

- the contract;
- work breakdown structure (WBS) and WBS dictionary;
- responsibility assignment matrix (RAM);
- statement of work (SoW);
- control account plan (CAP);
- work package authorisation.

Data traces steps to be performed

a. Determine the scope from the contract to be used for the data trace.
b. Determine the control account containing the trace item from (a) above, by reviewing the WBS and WBS dictionary.
c. Annotate the WBS and WBS dictionary pages to indicate the contract line item and deliverables that relate to the control account in (b) above.
d. Ensure that the control account (b) is assigned to a single responsible owner.
e. Review the work package authorisation documents for the control account that contains the trace item (b). Verify consistency in that the responsible owner in the work package authorisation documents is the same as the responsible owner in both the RAM and the control account.
f. Ensure that the work package authorisation documents are approved and signed by the responsible owner designated in the RAM.
g. Ensure that the scope is consistent in the work package authorisation and WBS dictionary.

13.2 Budget

The budget trace confirms that all the elements in the contract budget (Figure 4) consistently add to the contract price.

Where there are changes to the original contract, ensure that the changes have been tracked.

The hierarchy of budget elements is shown in Figure 4 below.

It is suggested that the following evidence be reviewed:

- work package authorisation;
- statement of work;
- work breakdown structure (WBS) and WBS dictionary.

Data trace steps to be performed

a. Select a control account to perform the data trace upon.
b. Ensure that the sum of the planning package budgets plus the work package budgets equals the control account budget for the trace item in (a) above.

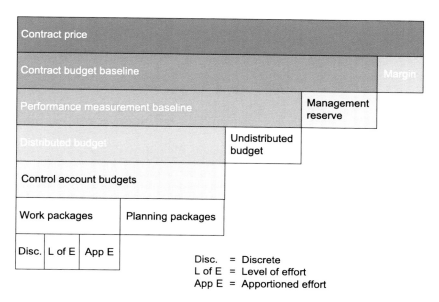

Figure 4 Contract budget elements

Modified from the *Earned Value Management: APM Guidelines* (2008).

c. Check for consistency and determine how control account budget values were established on the basis of estimate or purchase order (if applicable).

d. Review work package planning sheets and other performance measurement reports for the data trace item to determine if a tangible measurement technique is applied for assessing progress.

e. Verify that budget information in all internal and external performance reports align.

It is suggested the review checks that all budgets, from the control account budget through to the contract price, agree as per Figure 4.

13.3 Schedule

The schedule trace should establish a baseline has been set.

It is suggested that the following documents should be reviewed:

A Guide to Conducting Integrated Baseline Reviews (IBR)

- statement of work;
- project schedules;
- work package authorisation document.

Data trace steps to be performed

a. Determine the scope from the contract to be used for the data trace.
b. Confirm that all the schedules in Figure 5 contain the data trace item. Compare this against the statement of work for consistency.
c. Verify if the data trace item is logically linked to other appropriate packages.
d. Determine at which level the earned value will be captured, i.e. the performance measurement baseline. This will become the baseline schedule.
e. Check that the data trace item has a start and finish date on the baseline schedule.

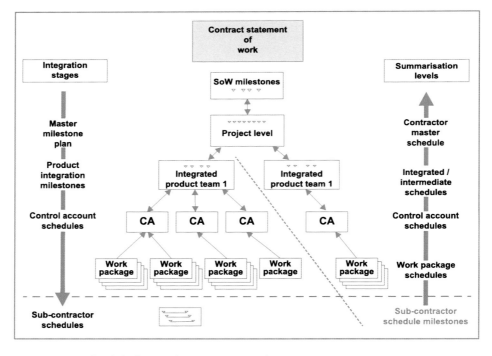

Figure 5 Schedule hierarchy integration diagram

Modified from the *Earned Value Management: APM Guidelines (2008)*.

f. Check for consistency of cost and durations on the control account documents with the budgeted cost for work scheduled (BCWS), start and finish dates on the baseline schedule and work package authorisation document.

g. Check that the schedule follows good scheduling practice (all work packages have predecessors and successors, minimal leads and lags, no negative float, no logic links on summary and justification for any constraints or tasks with high float).

13.4 Labour

The labour trace aims to understand how the direct labour costs are captured and transferred into the project control framework. The trace checks that the submission of an employee's timesheet flows through the accounting system and then into the performance measurement system. The timesheet error correction system/process should also be included in this particular trace.

Data trace steps to be performed

a. The trace should identify an individual transaction against a charge code in the control accounting for a particular period.

b. This should trace back to the completed employee's signed timesheet.

c. Check that this has been approved by a CAM, prior to entry into and out of the company accounting system.

The hourly cost rate should be applied to the hours booked to generate a total labour cost. This may take place in the accounting system or possibly in the performance measurement tool. The charge code may share its identity with the work package (WP). Further evidence will be the roll up of the WP(s) into the control account and to the actual cost of work performed (ACWP) appearing in the performance reports.

The timesheet error correction process/system should be included in this trace. Typically this should start with the CAM requesting a change to be made to an entry in the accounts or finance journal. The corrections to the control accounts should be approved by the CAM accepting the costs prior to entry into the accounting system. Where timesheets are electronic this may require re-approval by the CAM or their delegate. There should be a transaction showing the implemented correction.

13.5 Material

Material traces (that could include material, parts or sub-assemblies etc.) will vary considerably depending on the type of material(s) being used and the nature of the work being undertaken. A rough guide is that the detailed schedule should identify when the material has to be ordered, so it is available when required for use or integration.

Data trace steps to be performed

a. Select an item from the control account document which has a material requirement to be used for the data trace.
b. Find the work package that delivers this material.
c. Identify the work package on the schedule and check the dates are appropriate, i.e. the planned placing of the external commitment (purchase order) allows enough time for the material to be delivered ready for use.
d. Check that the internal commitment (purchase request) has been raised, and the values, qualities and timings are correct and authorised by the CAM. If the purchase order has been raised, check the values align to the purchase request.
e. Check the earned value techniques (EVTs) are appropriate for the material item.
f. Check the value in the schedule aligns to the control account.

If the project has been running for a length of time, these additional checks may be undertaken.

The procurement department or function will have raised a purchase order (PO) for materials. Find the PO for the data trace item. A price variance analysis can be carried out, comparing the order value with the budgeted price. If the material has been received, identify how the earned value was claimed.

13.6 Sub-contract management

The sub-contract management trace will verify the appropriate controls are in place and the schedules are integrated.

Data trace steps to be performed

a. Select an item from the control account document that has a sub-contract requirement to be used for the data trace.
b. Find the work package that relates to the sub-contract.
c. Identify the work package on the schedule and check the timings are aligned.
d. Check that the internal commitment (purchase request) has been raised, and the values, qualities and timings are correct and authorised by the CAM. If the purchase order has been raised, check the values align to the purchase request.
e. Check the earned value techniques (EVTs) are appropriate for the subcontract.
f. Check the value in the schedule aligns to the control account.

If the project has been running for a length of time, these additional checks may be undertaken.

The procurement department or function will have raised a purchase order (PO). Find the PO for the data trace item. A price variance analysis can be carried out, comparing the order value with the budgeted price. If the sub-contract has progressed, identify how the earned value was claimed.

13.7 Earned value

The earned value trace demonstrates the process for the collection of earned value status.

It is suggested that the following documents should be reviewed:

- project schedules;
- work package authorisation document.

The following checks may be undertaken:

a. Do the control accounts identify earned value techniques (EVTs) at work package level (or lower) to enable effective measurement of progress?
b. Review level of effort content of control account budgets to ensure it is only applied where appropriate. If possible obtain a summary of LoE work packages from the contractor.

c. Identify where the per cent complete EVT has been used and ensure that the CAM has appropriate rules of credit to prevent subjective progress measurement. There should be detailed tasks or work packages with identified discrete milestones.

d. Where progress has been claimed, is it in accordance with the EVT identified?

e. Check control account status sheets to ensure that progress is being claimed appropriately. For example, a 0–100% EVT package should have zero progress until it is complete.

13.8 Managerial analysis

This data trace will verify that the data is reliable and the information is useful for management decisions.

The following checks may be undertaken:

a. Is the estimate at completion (EAC) being updated and providing meaningful indication of the likely outcomes? This can be objective or subjective.
  - If an objective method is used, check it aligns with the earned value indicators as per the *EVM Guidelines* [2] and *EVM Handbook* [4].
  - If a subjective method is used, test the integrity of the method by taking into account the following:
    - past performance;
    - required efficiency to recover;
    - costs (incurred and committed) to date;
    - the use of contract charging rates (incorporating overhead cost pools) to obtain the cost of labour-based estimates;
    - technical assessment of tasks remaining;
    - cost and schedule variances incurred to date;
    - expected future efficiency;
    - percentage of task already completed and remaining risks (risk review and probability of cost impact);
    - ongoing or outstanding management actions;
    - forecast schedule completion of the task;
    - anticipated changes to the scope of work;
    - future economic conditions, forecast rate changes and escalation indices;
    - previous EAC trend.

b. Review variance analysis reports to ensure the following:
- Reasons for the variance are adequately explained (i.e. it should not simply say that there was a variance).
- Impact is identified, e.g. how it affects other control accounts and whether it affects the schedule overall.
- Corrective action or recovery plans are identified and are SMART (specific, measurable, achievable, realistic and time-bound).

c. Ensure that earned value reporting is being undertaken in accordance with the PCF.

13.9 Risk

The risk trace confirms that all risks (threats and opportunities) are recorded in the risk register, and that the approval process (if required) is correctly authorised and monitored.

It is suggested that the IBR Team should try to accomplish the following:

a. Confirm all risks are identified within the risk register.
b. Confirm that risks are being managed in accordance with the risk management plan (RMP). It is good practice to assign owners to each risk and their subsequent actions; this should be stated in the RMP.
c. Check any risk management actions are embedding into the baseline.
d. Are the risk management actions being progressed and monitored on a regular basis, in line with the RMP?

14

Annex C – Preparing for discussions

This check list should be used as a guide to support data scrub activities that may be undertaken in preparation for a CAM discussion.

Project specifics will demand that other checks are made in conjunction with the review of the wider project control framework against the selected standard.

14.1 Organisation charts

- Does the organisation chart correctly reflect the control account manager (CAM), CAM No. and control account title?
- Does the work breakdown structure (and/or related documentation/EV system) detail the control account work scope?

14.2 Control account plan

Figure 6 illustrates that work packages (WP) 1 to 3 are in an open status and would have cost collection numbers (CCN) because they have been planned prior to 'time now'. Once complete, WPs 1 to 3 would be closed to prevent incorrect/accidental bookings.

WP 4 has a closed status and no costs must be posted until 'time now' matches the WP start date because it is planned in the future.

A planning package (PP) always has a closed status for posting costs. It will be decomposed into WPs prior to the start date. Each of these WPs will be closed until 'time now' matches the WP start date.

- Does the status of all work packages and planning packages align with Figure 6?

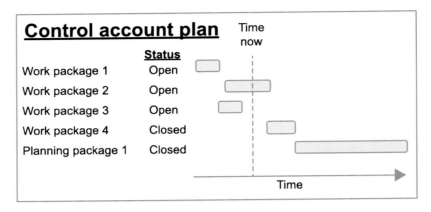

Figure 6 Control account plan

Reproduced with kind permission from the APM Planning, Monitoring and Control Specific Interest Group working group.

- Does the CAP adequately reference the CAM and relevant WBS/OBS elements?
- Are there any discrepancies between the WBS/OBS and control account/ control account plan references?
- Are the project references correct?
- Does the CAM name match that shown on the OBS chart?
- Does project documentation coding align with system data coding?
- Is the project name and/or reference shown?
- Are the project management plan, quality plan and contract master schedule documents referenced? Are they correct?
- Do the hours and monetary values at the control account level on the RAM/CA statement of work and budget allocation documents match those in the CAP?
- Do the breakdowns for other direct costs, materials and sub-contractor costs etc. match those approved at the summary level in the CAP?
- Do supporting pages and documents carry the same references as that of the CAP front sheet?
- Do all the work packages and planning packages have statements of work (SoW)?
- Do all the work and planning packages have budgets?
- Check for duplicate WBS numbers.
- Check the WBS roll up.

- Are WPs/PPs defined at an appropriate level in each project area?
- Check for duplicate packages (titles/SoWs).
- Do the values on the CA schedule match those in the CAP and the SoW?
- Do the schedule/project titles/activity names etc. correspond to the WBS?
- Are the earned value techniques (EVTs) appropriate and in line with planning guidelines (project instructions)?
- Review the methods the CAM is using to take earned value (EVTs). This may be shown on the control account plan or something similar. Any earned value being reported to the authority on the cost performance report (CPR), should be consistent and reconcilable to the internal earned value.
- Are the CAM, OBS and CAP correctly referenced on the schedule?

14.3 RAM

- Does the RAM detail the same WBS as the WBS and OBS charts?
- Are the titles the same?
- Do the money, items and hours match the CAP front sheet?

14.4 Contract master schedule

- Does the control account schedule reflect the requirements detailed on the contract master schedule?
- Does the CAM own any significant milestones?
- If so, are these contained within the control account schedule?
- If so, are they planned at the required date?

15

Annex D – Performing the review

15.1 Introduction

Depending on the organisational structure of the contractor, there may be value in conducting interviews with other personnel in the contractor's office, such as functional managers, team leaders and the project manager. The functional manager and team leader interviews will focus on their role with respect to the CAM regarding assistance with schedule, resourcing, review of risks and review of progress. These managers may be responsible for several CAMs.

The project manager interview will focus on risks, management reserve, reporting mechanisms within the contractor's office and the project manager's confidence in the PMB and the PCF. The project manager should provide details on the risk management structures and responsibilities and these should be verified through interviews with other managers.

An interview with the finance manager should be conducted to verify the manner in which overheads/indirect costs are applied to the contract.

The objective of these discussions is to enable the review team to understand the methods and reasoning for how the PMB has been developed, how it will be maintained and how performance data will be used to manage the project. The particular questions that should be asked should take account of the following:

- the structure of the particular project's control system;
- any risks/issues known to the review team prior to the review;
- any risks/issues identified from documentation reviews prior to the discussion.

Prior to each discussion, the review team should familiarise themselves with the following relating to the CAM in question:

- budgetary information from the RAM;
- control account definition and authorisation documents;
- work package definitions and associated budget structures;
- schedules;
- performance reports if available.

It is sometimes possible to use a dedicated portion of the review team to undertake pre-discussion 'data scrubs'. This entails an off-line review of the CAM folder, highlighting any areas of inconsistency or concern. This is documented and briefed to the review team member who has responsibility for the interview. A sample 'data scrub' checklist is provided in Annex B.

The number of CAM discussions to be conducted and the choice of CAMs and/or managers should be based on achieving an acceptable level of confidence that the sample is indicative of overall project performance. Particular attention should be given to any areas of the PMB or functional departments that the review team believes pose the greatest risk to the successful achievement of the project's objectives.

Discussions should be conducted in a non-adversarial manner and should be treated as a joint exercise for the benefit of both parties.

The discussion team should normally consist of no more than two representatives from the review team, one leading and asking the questions, the other taking notes and ensuring all areas have been covered. It is recommended that a representative from the project who has overall knowledge of the system be present as an observer to pick up any generic system issues. Where either the review team or project wish to add further observers, care should be taken not to detract from the objectives of the discussion or put either party in a position of unease. There may be occasions where the reviewers will need to include a technical peer to the CAM in the interview to test the basis of estimate, scheduling, budget and risk.

15.2 Creating the right environment for discussion

- Minimise external and internal distractions, do not allow your mind to wander off, keep focused on the speaker and turn off mobile phones.
- Where possible undertake the review in the interviewee's work area. This ensures a friendly environment and provides the opportunity for evidence not immediately to hand to be quickly located.

- Maintain eye contact to a level that you are both at ease.
- Squarely face the person, sit up straight, open your posture and relax.
- Lean slightly forward towards the person to show attentiveness through your body language.
- Focus solely on what the speaker is saying, try not to think of your next question, the interview will follow a logical path after the speaker makes their point.
- Keep an open mind, wait until the speaker finishes before considering if you agree or disagree. Try not to make assumptions about what the speaker is thinking.
- Respond appropriately to show you understand – murmur, nod, say words such as 'really' and 'interesting' and give direct prompts: 'what happens then?'.
- Engage yourself – ask questions for clarification but wait until the speaker is finished, that way you will not interrupt their chain of thought. After you ask a question paraphrase their response to ensure correct understanding.
- Avoid letting the speaker know how you handled a similar situation.
- Avoid close-ended questions that can be answered by 'yes' or 'no'. Phrase your questions so that they can be easily understood, and give the person being interviewed the opportunity to explain the process.
- Avoid using leading questions, i.e. one that infers a response.
- Use the 'show me' technique. Structure your discussion in such a manner to allow the interviewee enough 'room' to discuss freely how they follow the process. They should be encouraged to use reference material when answering questions. If they struggle to understand a question, try to rephrase without using jargon.
- If required, ask for relevant material to support their response. Where documentation is requested, but cannot be made available until after the discussion, be sure to get a commitment as to when you should receive it. This information is only to substantiate the interviewee's claim.
- Keep in mind your need to document your work and what is expected as adequate evidence of your conclusions. Take notes, and be comfortable with silence, whilst doing so.
- Remember you are looking for objective evidence, not fault finding. Most importantly, treat the interviewee like you would like to be treated if you were in the same situation.

15.3 After the discussion

Immediately following the discussion, the interview notes should be compiled into observations. It is recommended that reviewers maintain their own discussion files to keep notes for subsequent write-ups. You can then refer to them along with other data you may compile to complete the total write-up for your assigned review area. Follow-up on data requests if they are slow in being honoured.

The review team will review the key issues and if considered necessary, will present them to the project team to be resolved. It is the responsibility of the various review team members to ensure that they prepare a well-documented corrective action plan.

15.4 Themes

The following themes provide guidance on questions that may be asked during CAM discussions. For each theme, the intent and lines of enquiry are described through the remainder of the annex.

- business case;
- organisation;
- schedule, estimate and resourcing (labour and material);
- budgeting;
- sub-contract management;
- cost accounting;
- managerial analysis;
- change management;
- risk;
- behaviour/general – training, support, tools.

Business case

Intent

To confirm that the parameters, assumptions and constraints against which the project has to deliver are realistic and carry an appropriate level of risk. Make sure the objective output(s) of the business case are consistent with the project scope.

Lines of enquiry

- Alignment:
  - Establish that the project business case aligns with the programme business case, where applicable.
  - Determine if the business case includes a narrative explaining the affordability and deliverability of the project, i.e. is it realistically achievable within the given constraints?
  - Determine if the project scope, key dates and estimates align with the business case.
  - Ensure the cost profiles in the business case look reasonable and are consistent with the key activities and end dates in the schedule.
  - Establish that the qualitative and quantitative risk is aligned with the expectations of the business case.
  - Confirm that the risk management plan aligns with risk strategy in the business case.
- Document:
  - Ensure the review is against the latest approved business case.

Organisation

Intent

To test the interviewee's awareness and understanding of structures, i.e. the OBS, the WBS, the RAM, control accounts and work scope documentation, and to check that scope of work has been adequately covered.

Lines of enquiry

- Organisation breakdown structure:
  - Determine if all authorised work is assigned to organisational elements.
  - Is all the work in a control account assigned to just one CAM, and consistent with their area of expertise?
  - Are major sub-contractors included into the WBS/OBS?
  - Are roles, responsibility and accountabilities clearly defined and appropriate?
  - How are roles, responsibilities and accountabilities communicated across the project team?

- Work breakdown structure:
  - Determine if the WBS reflects the work to be performed.
  - Does the WBS cover everything to be delivered?
  - Where are the deliverables captured (e.g. in a WBS dictionary)?
  - Is there a clear link to the contract requirements and how is this captured?
- Responsibility assignment matrix:
  - Determine for each intersection of the WBS and OBS, a single control account is visible, and a CAM is assigned.
  - Determine if each CAM understands what they are responsible for and the boundary of their scope.
  - Do the CAMs understand the value of their workload?
  - Have the resources required to do the work been identified?
- Control account/work package documentation:
  - Does the WBS extend to the control account level?
  - Have the CAMs got delegated authority to deliver their scope of work?
  - Is the CAMs' scope of work clearly defined (with clear deliverables etc.)?
  - Are sub-contracted elements clearly identified?

Schedule, estimate and resourcing

Intent

To test the CAM's understanding of the various schedules, the interfaces between them, the quality of the schedules and if they are achievable. To gain an appreciation of the resourcing studies that have been done and the needs identified, including understanding of whether people are working reasonable hours. To identify risk management activities in CAM schedules. To ensure that appropriate earned value techniques (EVTs) are being used and assess if the schedule is achievable.

Lines of enquiry

- The schedule:
  - Can the CAM explain how the tasks in the schedule meet the deliverables in contact?
  - Is the schedule realistically achievable, i.e. has it been benchmarked against similar projects, or used estimating norms?

- Did the CAM build their schedule or did they inherit it. If they inherited it, do they have any concerns about its deliverability? Do they understand it?
- How does the schedule interface with related schedules either vertically (e.g. delivering contract milestones), or horizontally (i.e. dependencies across control accounts)?
- Check there is an appropriate mix of work packages (short term) and planning packages (long term).
- Has the scheduling maturity model [3] been used to assess the quality and maturity of the schedule quality?
- Has the schedule been baselined?
■ Basis of estimates:
- How did they arrive at the estimates used in the schedule (e.g. use of estimating norms, benching against other similar projects etc.)?
- Where is basis of estimate recorded?
- Is the split between labour and material clear?
■ Resources:
- Is there sufficient committed resource to deliver the schedule?
- What are the utilisation assumptions (including overtime)?
- Does the resource histogram look appropriate, i.e. smoothed?
■ Assumptions:
- What are the schedule assumptions?
- Where are they recorded?
- Are unstable or critical assumptions backed by risks within the risk register?
■ Earned value techniques:
- Has the APM *Earned Value Management Handbook* [4] been followed? (For further information see Section 4.22 of the APM *Earned Value Management Handbook*.)
- Have the EVTs been applied to the schedule at the correct level, i.e. work package?
- Check the volume for level of effort is appropriate (see *EVM Handbook*).
■ Schedule progress collection:
- How is progress captured?
- How frequently?
■ Schedule analysis:
- How is the schedule analysed (e.g. critical path analysis (CPA), milestone tracking etc.)?
■ Supplier schedules:
- See sub-contract management lines of enquiry.

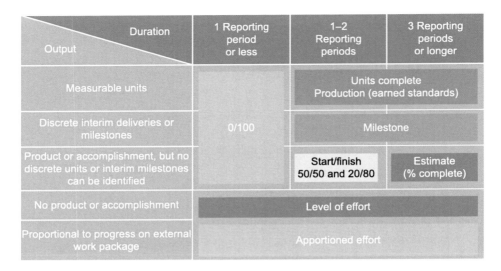

	Duration	1 Reporting period or less	1–2 Reporting periods	3 Reporting periods or longer
Output				
Measurable units			Units complete Production (earned standards)	
Discrete interim deliveries or milestones		0/100	Milestone	
Product or accomplishment, but no discrete units or interim milestones can be identified			Start/finish 50/50 and 20/80	Estimate (% complete)
No product or accomplishment		Level of effort		
Proportional to progress on external work package		Apportioned effort		

Figure 7 Earned value techniques (EVT)

Taken from the APM *Earned Value Management Handbook* (2013).

Budgeting

Intent

To test whether the budgeting system shows that there is sufficient budget to cover the full scope and duration of the project. The budget system has to be integrated with the project's schedules and able to plan earned value and record actual earned value.

Lines of enquiry

- Determine if all work packages (WP) within a control account have:
  - a baselined budget value;
  - a baseline value that has been phased in line with the earned value technique;
  - an alignment with the work packages' baselined dates.
- Determine that all planning packages (PP) have a budget and the sum of work packages and planning packages equate to the control account authorised budget.

- Gain an understanding of whether the budget is sufficient for the tasks to be undertaken through discussion of risks/assumptions/schedule.
- Understand the following budget values:
  - level of effort tasks;
  - split between WPs and PPs;
  - split between labour and materials;
  - amount of sub-contract.
- Determine how management reserve has been generated, who owns it and how it is used.
- Understand how undistributed budgets are controlled.
- Understand the process for how budget is earned (budgeted cost of work performed (BCWP)) and collected; to include labour, sub-contract and materials.

Sub-contract

Intent

To test that work being performed by sub-contractors has been incorporated into the project's baseline with appropriate collection of actual/forecast data taking place.

Lines of enquiry

- Control account work package documentation:
  - Determine if the major sub-contractors have been identified in the project documentation and structures (e.g. OBS, WBS dictionary, CAPs etc.).
  - Ascertain how sub-contract schedules have been incorporated into the control account schedules and meet the master schedule requirements.
  - Look for evidence that sub-contractors' costs have been scrutinised and included in the control account's budget baseline.
  - Determine whether the CAM has used an appropriate earned value technique (EVT) for measuring performance and kept any level of effort work to a minimum.
- Process:
  - Determine how the collection of actual cost and actual performance from sub-contractors is done and assess for timeliness and accuracy.
  - Review frequency of sub-contractor estimated completion dates and estimated costs are adequate.

Cost collection (accounting)

Intent

To test that cost collection codes exist for all planned work, and that costs for labour and purchases are being made in an accurate and timely manner.

Lines of enquiry

- Determine how the direct costs are booked (labour and material).
- Determine how you get visibility of the costs attributable to your CA. This will include indirect costs and journal transfers.
- Determine how the system ensures that the costs booked to your account are accurate.
- Determine how you would rectify a mistake.
- Determine who else is involved in the cost collection process.
- Determine that the cost situation is reported. Who looks at it? How is it reviewed/authorised?
  - cash flow;
  - authority to spend;
  - budget allocation;
  - commitment values;
  - PO management process.
- Review whether the project uses accruals or 'estimated actual costs' to avoid artificial cost variances and how these are managed.
- Determine how would you assure yourself that contractor applications for payments are reasonable and in line with contractual expectations.
- Determine how you ensure that you have received all costs before closing packages of work. Refer to disallowable costs, invoices on hold and not paid, disputes on quality and deliverables. Matching POs to invoices.
- Determine how you would stop work.

Managerial analysis

Intent

To test that the managerial analysis and reporting requirements are being met, and the content of the report is appropriate and understood by the interviewee. To ensure that reports produced are accurate, add value and any variances are acted upon.

Lines of enquiry

- Reporting:
  - Identify what performance information is generated or received.
  - Ensure budgets, earned value and actual costs are reported in terms of labour, material and other direct costs.
  - Check that the frequency of the report generated is appropriate (typically at least monthly).
  - Check who receives the reports. What level of management gets EV-based reporting?
  - Check their understanding of the report content (e.g. do they know how much has been spent, are they on, behind or ahead of schedule, do they understand why?).
- Variances:
  - Test their understanding of the variance thresholds of their control accounts and how they will know when this has been exceeded.
  - If they are not on track, do they understand the consequences to the project of what will happen, and what action they need to take?
  - Determine that variance reports show a statement of the problem, the variance, its cause and impact, and proposed corrective action.
- Action Plans:
  - Demonstrate how plans are approved.
  - Demonstrate how corrective action plans are tracked to ensure they are carried out in a timely manner.
- Forecasting:
  - Determine how cost and schedule forecasting is completed (e.g. Estimate to Complete (ETC) and EAC and forecast dates).
  - Determine frequency of when EAC is revised and check it is appropriate.
  - When and where are forecasts formally incorporated into an EAC?

Change management

Intent

To test whether the interviewee (typically the control account manager or project manager) has an understanding of the change management process, and to understand whether the processes are being applied appropriately.

Lines of enquiry

- Does the interviewee know where to find the change management process?
- Can the interviewee demonstrate their understanding of this process?
- Determine whether changes are being authorised for the right reasons.
- Determine if project changes have applied the process correctly.
- Determine if changes are made in a timely manner to avoid retroactive changes.
- Ensure changes are correctly authorised.
- Ensure the change log is updated in line with the process.
- Can the original budget be reconciled to the current budget?
- Ensure that the hierarchy of budget elements as described in Figure 4, has incorporated all changes and is arithmetically correct.
- Determine if authorised changes have resulted in changes to the appropriate project documentation.
  - For example, but not restricted to, WBS, WBS dictionary, lists of deliverables, control account authorisations, statement of works, project management plan etc.
- Determine if the change has resulted in a change to the control account plans' detailed schedules.

Risk

Intent

To test the interviewee's understanding of the risk management process, including how they identify, assess and plan responses to risks. To ensure that the existing responses are appropriately controlled (budgeted within the schedule) and ensure that the process to manage future risk responses is understood and funding exists.

Lines of enquiry

- Risk management process:
  - Do they understand the process and associated terminology?
  - How is management reserve (MR) governed and applied on your control account?
  - How have you provisioned for the transfer of residual risk at control account completion?

- Risks:
  - Do they know what the top project risks are, and are they appropriate?
  - Demonstrate what risk management actions are within their schedule.
  - Do they feel the project adequately understands its cost, schedule and technical risk?
- Risk analysis:
  - Determine their knowledge of risk analysis (quantitative and qualitative).
  - Determine how allowance has been made for risk in baseline estimates.
  - Confirm that risks held in the register do not duplicate the allowance.
  - Determine how risks are escalated.

Behaviour/general

Intent

To test the environmental factors that have been put in place to encourage and support the successful delivery of the project.

Lines of enquiry

- Training/competence development:
  - What training is there for project staff, CAMs and senior managers involved in the project or its controls?
  - How is their competence assessed for their roles?
- Support from management:
  - What level of support is received from senior management?
  - Investigate if the information provided by project controls is actually used.
  - Determine examples of how recovery actions were supported.
  - Demonstrate how good practice is encouraged and rewarded.
  - How would bad news/unfavourable variances be received?
- Strength of function:
  - What level of support is received from the functions (project management, finance, commercial etc.) to ensure that the project succeeds?
- Strength of process:
  - Is the process comprehensive?
  - Do people understand their roles in project control?

A Guide to Conducting Integrated Baseline Reviews (IBR)

- Effectiveness of toolsets:
  - Does the toolset support or hinder delivery of the project (data received on time, simple to make changes etc.)?
  - What control does the project have over the toolset? And is it appropriate?
- Customer:
  - Is there an open, collaborative relationship with the customer?

Glossary

Acceptance criteria A prioritised set of criteria that the project product must meet before the customer will accept it, i.e. measurable definitions of the attributes required for the set of products to be acceptable to key stakeholders.

Activity An element of work performed during the course of a project. An activity normally has an expected duration, an expected cost and expected resource requirements. Activities are often subdivided into tasks.

Actual cost of work performed (ACWP) The costs actually incurred and recorded in accomplishing the work performed within a given time period.

Authorised work That effort which has been defined and is on contract plus that effort for which contract costs have not been agreed to but for which written authorisation has been received.

Baseline See Performance measurement baseline.

Benefit The measurable improvement resulting from an outcome perceived as an advantage by one or more stakeholders.

Budget The resources (in money and/or hours) assigned for the accomplishment of a specific task or group of tasks.

Budgeted cost for work performed (BCWP) The value of completed work. This is the sum of the budgets for completed work packages and completed portions of open work packages, plus the applicable portion of the budgets for level of effort and apportioned effort. See Earned value.

Budgeted cost for work scheduled (BCWS) The planned value of the work to be done. This is the sum of the budgets for all work packages, planning packages etc., scheduled to be accomplished (including in-process work packages), plus the amount of level of effort and apportioned effort scheduled to be accomplished within a given time period.

Change control A process that ensures that all changes made to a project's baseline scope, time, cost or quality objectives are identified, evaluated, approved, rejected or deferred.

Glossary

Control account (CA)   A management control point at which actual costs can be accumulated and compared to budgeted cost for work performed. A control account is a natural control point for cost/schedule planning and control since it represents the work assigned to one responsible organisational element on one work breakdown structure (WBS) element.

Control account manager (CAM)   The manager who is responsible for planning, performing and monitoring the elements of work defined within a control account.

Control account plans (CAP)   A group of documents that identify the scope of work and how it will be delivered within the defined cost and time parameters.

Cost collection numbers (CCN)   A booking number or finance code allocated to collect labour, material and other direct costs against the baseline plan, at a level determined by the organisation.

Cost performance report (CPR)   A contractually required report, prepared by the company, containing information derived from the internal system. Provides status of progress on the contract.

Cost variance (CV)   A metric for the cost performance of a project. It is the algebraic difference between the earned value and the actual cost (CV = BCWP − ACWP).

Critical path (CP)   A sequence of activities through a project network or schedule from start to finish, the sum of whose durations determines the overall project duration. There may be more than one such path. The path through a series of activities, taking into account interdependencies, in which the late completion activities will have an impact on the project end date or delay a key milestone.

Customer   The person or group who commissioned the work and will benefit from the end results.

Data trace   A data trace is a methodology for tracing a source data element through the project control framework (PCF).

Deliverable (or output)   A specialist product that is handed over to the user(s).

Earned value (EV)   The value of completed work expressed in terms of the budget assigned to that work. See BCWP.

Earned value management (EVM) A best practice project control process that is based on a structured approach to planning, cost collection and performance measurement. It facilitates the integration of project scope, schedule, cost, risk and resource objectives and the establishment of a baseline plan for performance measurement.

Earned value techniques (EVT) Methods of objectively measuring earned value.

Estimate An approximation of project time and cost targets, refined throughout the project life cycle.

Estimate at completion (EAC) Actual direct costs, plus indirect costs allocable to the contract, plus the estimate of costs (direct and indirect) for authorised work remaining.

Estimate to complete (ETC) The forecast of labour hours and costs required to complete the remaining authorised work. It is based on a bottom-up analysis of remaining work and consideration of past and future performance is taken into consideration.

Integrated baseline review (IBR) A process to enable a technical and schedule review to establish visibility into the maturity of the planning and execution. The focus of the review is on the assignment, definition, scheduling, integration and resourcing of work.

Level of effort (LoE) Effort of a general or supportive nature which does not produce definite end products.

Management reserve (MR) An amount of the total allocated budget withheld for management control purposes rather than designated for the achievement of a specific task or set of tasks. It is not a part of the performance measurement baseline. Also known as contingency.

Milestone An activity of zero duration principally used to enhance the clarity of the programme structure.

Organisational breakdown structure (OBS) A hierarchical way in which an organisation may be divided into management levels and groups, for planning and control purposes.

Performance measurement baseline (PMB) The time-phased budget plan against which contract performance is measured. It is formed by the budgets assigned to control accounts and the applicable indirect budgets. For future effort, not planned to the control account level, the performance measurement baseline also includes budgets assigned to higher level WBS elements, and undistributed budgets. It equals the total allocated budget less management reserve (MR).

Planned value (PV)   See Budgeted cost for work scheduled.

Planning   The process of identifying the means, resources and actions necessary to accomplish an objective.

Planning package (PP)   A budget for future work that is not yet practical to plan at the work package (WP) level.

Project controls   The application of processes to measure project perform-ance against the project plan, to enable variances to be identified and corrected, so that project objectives are achieved.

Project controls framework (PCF)   A document that identifies the processes, guidance, key roles, reports and reviews for using project controls for: cost and schedule management; performance measurement; project execution. Where earned value is applied this may be known as the earned value management system description (EVMSD).

Project lead   The person leading the review on behalf of the project.

Responsibility assignment matrix (RAM)   A depiction of the relation-ship between the contract work breakdown structure elements and the organisa-tions assigned responsibility for ensuring their accomplishment.

Review sponsor   The person who initiates the review.

Risk response (mitigation action)   Actions that may be taken to bring a situation to a level where exposure to risk is acceptable to the organisation. These responses fall into a number of risk response categories.

Rules of credit   Criteria used to determine the progress of work done.

Schedule   A schedule is the timetable for a project. It shows how project activities and milestones are planned over a period of time. It is often shown as either a milestone chart, Gantt chart or other bar chart, or a tabulated series of dates.

Schedule variance (SV)   A metric for the schedule performance on a programme. It is the difference between the earned value and the planned value (schedule variance = earned value – planned value). A positive value is a favourable condition while a negative value is unfavourable.

Scheduling The process used to determine the overall project duration. This includes identification of activities and their logical dependencies, and estimating activity durations, taking into account requirements and availability of resources. Not to be confused with planning.

Stakeholder Any individual, group or organisation that can affect, be affected by, or perceive itself to be affected by, an initiative (programme, project, activity, risk).

Statement of work (SoW) A narrative description of products or services to be delivered by the project (source: APM Body of Knowledge).

Supplier The person, group or groups responsible for the supply of the project's specialist products.

Terms of reference The scope of the review.

Undistributed budget (UB) Budget applicable to contract effort that has not yet been identified to WBS elements at, or below, the lowest level of reporting to the government.

Variances Those differences between planned and actual performance that require further review, analysis or action. Thresholds should be established as to the magnitude of variances that will require variance analysis, and the thresholds should be revised as needed to provide meaningful analysis during execution of the contract.

Work breakdown structure (WBS) The complete work breakdown structure for a contract, it includes the contractually approved work breakdown structure for reporting purposes and its discretionary extension to the lower levels by the company, in accordance with the contract. It includes all the elements for the hardware, software, data or services that are the responsibility of the company.

Work package (WP) Detailed short-span jobs, or material items, identified by the company for accomplishing work required to complete the contract.

Work package planning sheets Documentation that captures the breakdown of a control account into work packages and planning packages, outlining the basis of cost and schedule estimates and the proposed earned value techniques.

Abbreviations and acronyms

ACWP	Actual cost of work performed
APM	Association for Project Management
BCWP	Budget cost for work performed
BCWS	Budget cost for work scheduled
CA	Control account
CAM	Control account manager
CAP	Control account plan
CCN	Cost collection numbers
CPA	Critical path analysis
CPR	Cost performance report
EAC	Estimate at completion
ETC	Estimate to complete
EVM	Earned value management
EVMSD	Earned value management system description
EVT	Earned value techniques
LFE	Learning from experience
LoE	Level of effort
MR	Management reserve
OBS	Organisational breakdown structure
PCF	Project control framework
PMB	Performance measurement baseline
PMO	Programme management office
PO	Purchase order
PP	Planning package
RAM	Responsibility assignment matrix
RMP	Risk management plan
SIG	Specific interest group
SoW	Statement of work

Abbreviations and acronyms

SV   Schedule variance
WBS   Work breakdown structure
WP   Work package

References

1 Association for Project Management (2010) *The Earned Value Management Compass*. ISBN: 978-1-903494-33-2.
2 Association for Project Management (2008) *Earned Value Management: APM Guidelines*. ISBN: 978-1-903494-26-4.
3 Association for Project Management (2011) *The Scheduling Maturity Model*. ISBN: 978-1-903494-26-4.
4 Association for Project Management (2013) *Earned Value Management Handbook*. ISBN: 978-1-903494-47-9.

Bibliography

Association for Project Management (2008) *Interfacing Risk and Earned Value Management*. ISBN: 978-1-903494-24-0.

Association for Project Management (2008) *Introduction to Project Planning*. ISBN: 978-1-903494-28-8.

Association for Project Management (2010) *Introduction to Project Control*. ISBN: 978-1-903494-34-9.

Index

Index

Index